9-30-77

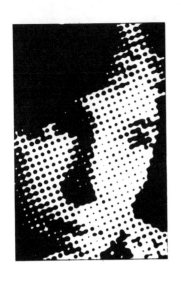

SPECIAL EDUCATION CAREERS

SPECIAL EDUCATION CAREERS

Training the Handicapped Child

Theodore Huebener, Ph.D.

FRANKLIN WATTS
NEW YORK | LONDON | 1977

Acknowledgements

Mrs. Desoyza at These Our Treasures; Miss Samuels at the New York Philanthropic League; Mrs. O'Neill and Mr. Conti at The Lighthouse, The New York Association for the Blind.

Photographs courtesy of: Chuck Freedman: pp. ii, viii, 4, 9, 15, 24, 25, 28, 31, 36, 37, 40, 46, 47, 49. Wide World Photos: p. 13. Pre-College Programs of Gallaudet College: pp. 19 (top), 43. Board of Education, The City of New York, Bureau of Audio-Visual Instruction: pp. 18 (top and bottom), 19 (bottom).

Library of Congress Cataloging in Publication Data

Huebener, Theodore, 1895–
    Special education careers.

    (A Career concise guide)
    Includes index.
    SUMMARY: Discusses the rewards and difficulties of working with handicapped children, and describes professional duties, techniques, and job opportunities in this field.
    1. Handicapped children—Education—Juvenile literature. [1. Handicapped children—Education—Vocational guidance. 2. Vocational guidance] I. Title.
LC4015.H83   371.9   77–6298
ISBN 0–531–01311–1

Contents

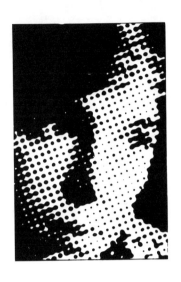

SPECIAL EDUCATION CAREERS

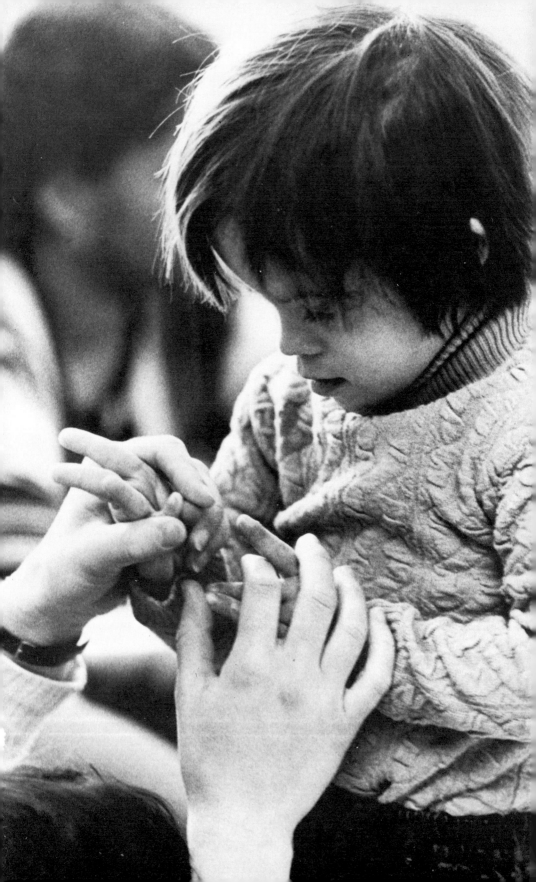

Introduction

In choosing a vocation, there are a number of things you ought to consider besides pay. Since you want to be happy in your work, the most important question is: Do you like the daily activities you would be involved in? Are you eager to make this vocation your life career? You should ask: Is it important? Is it highly regarded?

If you are thinking of teaching, the answer to the last two questions is definitely yes! Teaching has great cultural and social importance for the community as well as for the individual.

As a profession, teaching enjoys several unique advantages. In daily contact with children, a teacher lives in an environment of youth. Colleagues are educated, cultured people who are dealing, even in a modest way, with the treasures of our accumulated wisdom and knowledge. The material advantages of teaching, too, are attractive, with a long summer vacation, rather good pay, and a pension.

Of the various areas of teaching, one of the most interesting and important is the education of the handicapped child. This is now a regular part of every well-organized school system. It is, in fact, considered of major importance.

The federal government is giving Special Education its moral and financial support. The appropriation for the Division of Special Education in New York is about $367 million per year. Ten percent of the funds for vocational education are allotted to Special Education. There are about eight million handicapped children in the United States.

Even though there have been substantial reductions in school expenditures, and a number of teaching areas have been reduced, a decline in programs for the handicapped is unlikely. There is every indication that they will continue to expand.

Working with Handicapped Children

When Gladys Tobin first entered a class of handicapped children, she was actually disgusted. Although their handicaps did not seem to disturb the children very much, she got the impression that they were wild and unruly.

In dealing with an abnormal situation or person, the first reaction is often an unfavorable one. A lot of patience and a friendly attitude will overcome most of the difficulties. Gladys found that after working with the children for awhile, the handicaps seemed less disturbing. The important thing was to value each child for what he or she could do and to build up a feeling of self-confidence.

Handicapped pupils learn how to express themselves creatively through puppetry. Through dancing and moving about, they learn creative expression, and through physical training and therapy, they improve their coordination. Speech and language are improved with special training. The children also take on personal

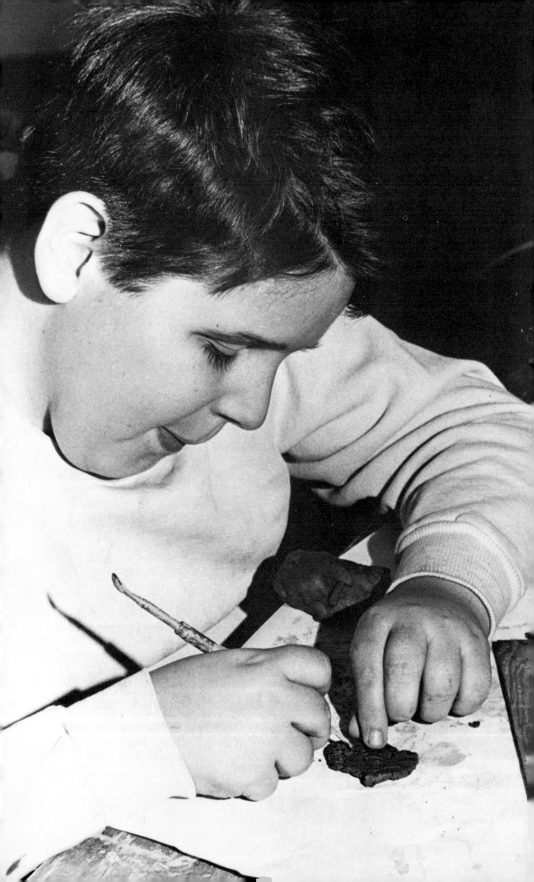

responsibilities, and this builds up pride in their achievement.

Puppetry is especially effective for teaching language, inspiring creativity, and helping children learn how to get along with one another. Gladys finds that the children really enjoy it. A typical lesson is very basic and simple.

A pupil with a puppet on each hand may make the two puppets nod to one another and say, "Hello! How are you?" Another child may make his two puppets clap or wrestle, to amuse other youngsters lying on the floor watching the "show."

Gladys takes part in this kind of "game" also. For instance, she may use a large cardboard figure to act out a simple role. She may skip around saying, "I'm a little girl!" Then she will give cardboard figures to the pupils, who will put them on and act out roles of who they are or would like to be. In connection with puppetry, there is a lot of free activity which the children enjoy, and, even though they can't talk clearly, they feel encouraged to speak.

With patience and understanding, Gladys helps the children become cooperative members of the group. One boy, who in the beginning tried to hit Gladys and swore at her, eventually came to admire her and love her. To express their emotion, the children often hug and kiss the teacher.

A physically handicapped
student works on clay with
modeling tools at the
New York Philanthropic League.

What pleases Gladys most, however, is that through her influence the children have learned to help one another. She has encouraged them in their social progress and created an atmosphere of joyful activity. As Gladys expresses it, "All children, no matter how mentally or physically handicapped, are capable of learning—it just takes longer. First we break a learning task down into very simple, basic steps. You have to be very flexible and imaginative. You're always studying and working out fresh approaches, especially since no two children are alike or respond in the same way. Sometimes I do get tired or frustrated, but as each step is successfully completed, I don't know who feels more thrilled, the child or me."

The Handicapped Child

In the field of education, the term "Special Education" refers to the training of handicapped children—children with special needs. Special Education may also refer to gifted children. This book, however, deals with the handicapped child. The largest single area of Special Education is that of "physically handicapped" children. (These don't include children with limited vision or hearing; they are included in a category of their own.) Larger school systems classify physically handicapped children under the following categories: those who require health conservation, those who need home instruction, brain-damaged children, children with severe orthopedic defects, and hospitalized patients.

Handicapped children are "uncovered" in various ways. Normally, a handicapped child is assigned to a special school or class after a doctor, a psychologist, or a therapist has recognized the handicap. Sometimes handicaps are obvious; sometimes they are discovered by mere chance.

Since children are handicapped in different ways, there is a great variety of programs for them. The visually handicapped and those with poor hearing usually go to special classes with specially trained teachers. Children with only slight handicaps may attend regular classes. Multiple-handicapped children—that is, children who are blind or deaf and also mentally retarded —have special classes with special activities designed to meet their needs.

Another special area is that of socially maladjusted and emotionally disturbed children. Severely disturbed children go to special schools; milder cases are provided for in regular classes with the service of a resource teacher. The aim is to return the children to the mainstream of education as soon as possible.

In all these areas, the children are taught by specially licensed teachers, supported by *itinerant* and *resource* teachers, psychologists, and social workers.

There are basically two schools of thought about educating handicapped children. One approach is to place them in classes of their own. Another approach, fast gaining in popularity, is to "mainstream" handicapped children—that is, to place them as often as possible in regular classes with normal children.

Those who prefer segregation argue that a handicapped child is happier and makes better progress when placed in a group of similarly handicapped children, taught by one teacher.

A teacher gives her
full attention to helping this
brain-damaged child
acquire a basic motor skill.

Others feel that it is more effective and wholesome to educate handicapped children together with normal children. This group feels that special rooms may be provided for handicapped children, but they should take all the regular subjects that they possibly can with normal children.

In what are called "sight-saving" programs, the non-segregation policy is preferred. The hard-of-hearing child, too, is often placed in a classroom with normal pupils, but also receives special classes in lipreading and speech correction.

Because they need so much special attention, crippled, undernourished, and cardiac children are usually segregated. In the past, mentally handicapped children have generally been segregated, but that is changing, especially when a child is fairly well adjusted socially. In some cities special schools exist for one type of handicapped child only. The most common practice, however, is to have special classes for the handicapped in schools for normal pupils. Then the handicapped children can join in the many social functions in which the whole school participates.

Teachers
of the
Handicapped

The teacher of the handicapped has an interesting and challenging job, for he or she also teaches the usual elementary and secondary school subjects—reading, writing, spelling, arithmetic, history, geography, science, drawing, and music, together with various types of handicrafts. These include clay modeling, weaving, basketry, metalwork and woodwork, sewing, and cooking.

Children who do woodwork and metalwork learn the care of tools and materials like wood, paints, varnish, and wax. The teacher becomes an amateur carpenter, metalworker, and painter.

The use of visual aids is of great importance in the teaching of the academic subjects, as well as of handicrafts. This means that the teacher should know how to letter, prepare signs and charts, make outline drawings, and arrange exhibits.

The wide variety of activities makes teaching the handicapped interesting and enjoyable. Success depends, of course, on the imagination and resourcefulness of the teacher, who has to be a person of many skills.

After several years of experience, a teacher may become a supervisor or coordinator. The supervisor observes and evaluates the classroom activities of the teachers. The coordinator is mainly concerned with building up a curriculum, developing new procedures, and supplying appropriate materials.

Requirements for the license to teach the handicapped include a college degree and courses in education, elementary school methods, child psychology, and supervised teaching. Additional special requirements for different teaching jobs are given in the chapters that follow.

The salary range for teachers in the field of Special Education is from $9,000 to $20,000.

TEACHER OF HEALTH CONSERVATION

Health conservation classes are for children who are physically incapacitated or weak, but still can get around without too much difficulty. Severe cases go to hospitals or convalescent homes. There they take the regular elementary subjects, taught by itinerant teachers.

It is important to create a comfortable physical and mental environment for the children. Most classes are held on the ground floor, so as to avoid stair-climbing.

A seventh-grade general science class in a school for physically handicapped, but mentally normal children.

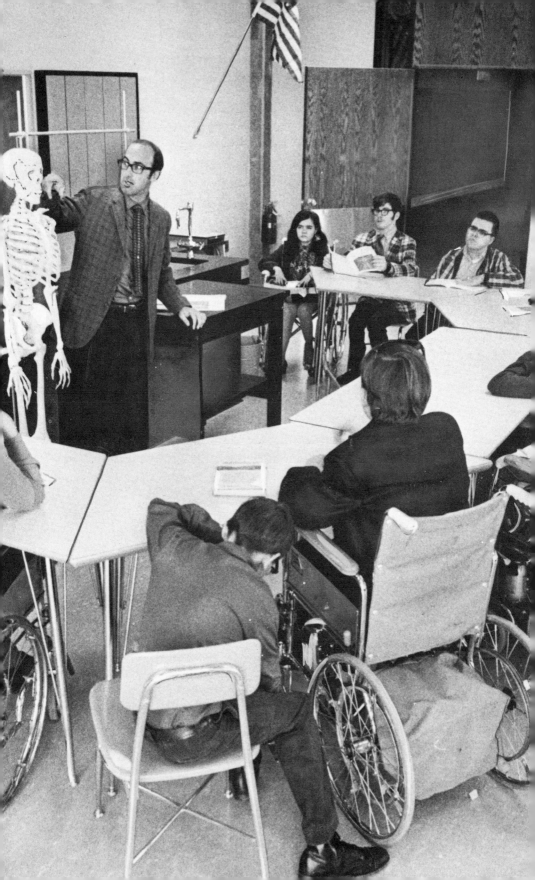

During the day, there are rest periods and snack periods, so the children may relax. Special attention is given to the food served, and the children receive some elementary education in nutrition. These children also need help in making adjustments to physical disabilities. The teacher often works with groups of children who have a common physical problem. The games and recreational activities are adjusted to the capacities of each child.

Requirements for a license of teacher of health conservation include a B.A. degree and some practice teaching physically handicapped children. You will also take courses to help you understand physically handicapped children and their special needs.

TEACHER OF THE VISUALLY HANDICAPPED

Since there are different problems of eyesight, there are many different programs for the visually handicapped. Children with only mild problems of eyesight go to regular classes; they are able to use printed materials and move about without difficulty. They also get extra help from resource teachers.

Children who are practically blind may also take the regular school curriculum, but they have to have special learning materials that use the senses of touch and hearing rather than sight. These are provided in a resource room. Special classes are held for children with more than one handicap. These pupils may be men-

---

A visually handicapped child enjoys her harmonica during a musical session at the Lighthouse, a part of the New York Association for the Blind.

tally retarded or emotionally disturbed in addition to having poor vision. "Paraprofessionals"—helpers who have less training than fully licensed teachers—often give extra help to these children.

Itinerant teachers help children who aren't succeeding in the regular program or for whom it is physically impossible to be in a regular class. An itinerant teacher goes wherever he or she is needed and teaches in several different places each day. There is an itinerant teacher assigned to each case to teach and to help decide what program will be best for the child.

Visually handicapped pupils in resource programs follow the same curriculum as their classmates in the regular class, using the special materials provided by the resource teacher. The blind child has to learn Braille for reading. Braille is a system of using raised dots that stand for letters. By running the fingers over these dots the blind person can "read" by using the sense of touch rather than sight. He or she will also have to learn the Nemeth Code, which is an adaptation of Braille to mathematics. The teacher also helps the child learn how to move around more confidently.

The visually limited pupil may need the help of various optical aids, large-print materials, readers, or recorded material to function satisfactorily in his regular class.

Cheryl is typical of the student who benefits from the use of these resources. Cheryl speaks clearly and writes neatly. But she has to hold her face close to the paper to read or write. Her vision is clouded, although she can see well enough for ordinary purposes.

In a half-hour lesson after her regular class, Cheryl shows the resource teacher her homework assignment in math. It requires the identifying of numbers within various sets and describing the sets. There are many technical terms that Cheryl has to define—"brace," "set," "element," "cardinal," and so on.

The teacher writes out these expressions, which are then enlarged on a machine. Cheryl will take the material home and study it. There she will also use an enlarger or a magnifying glass.

Cheryl also uses a machine called a "visual tech" that looks like a TV set. When she puts her reader in an opening below, the printed page appears on the screen in enlarged form. She can read this without difficulty, and as she reads aloud, the teacher corrects a few mispronunciations. This extra help makes it possible for Cheryl to handle regular classwork in spite of her poor vision.

The requirements for a license to teach children with limited vision are a B.A. degree and additional specialized courses. These include courses dealing with the nature and needs of the visually handicapped; physical, clinical, and medical factors relating to eye conditions; curriculum adaptation for the blind; methods of teaching; materials and equipment; and basic skill in reading and writing Braille.

TEACHER OF THE DEAF AND HARD-OF-HEARING

The teacher of the hard-of-hearing in the lower school has a background in elementary education, early childhood education, and speech improvement. At first, the

---

Overleaf: Deaf children need to be helped to make the language sounds they cannot hear. Teachers of speech and speech therapy are working attentively with these deaf and hard-of-hearing children.

emphasis is on hearing acutely and speaking correctly. Later, reading and writing skills are developed and the child studies the usual elementary school subjects. Teachers of speech or speech therapy do individual therapy for pupils who need it.

Occasionally, deaf and "language-impaired" children can get along in a regular class with the help of a special teacher. They are integrated into the system. The special teacher provides outside instruction and guidance. Hard-of-hearing children also have special classes in lipreading and auditory training that teaches them how to make the best of the hearing they have.

Lipreading and oral work go hand in hand. A deaf child is taught to read by beginning with the mouth; first he or she learns to speak correctly. Much is done with toys, games, and physical activities. The teacher uses many special techniques. For example, deaf children may be helped to pronounce words by feeling the vibrations the sounds produce. Practicing with a boy named Mario, for example, his teacher, Ellen, kneels close to him so that their faces are on the same level. She places Mario's hands on her face so he can feel the sound vibrate while she says the M–sound: "Mm . . . mmm . . . Mario." Then Mario tries to say his name the same way, feeling the vibration in his own face as well as imitating the position of Ellen's lips and mouth. Teachers like Ellen learn a great many different techniques which they combine and use constantly.

Two general approaches are used to teach the hard-of-hearing. One places sole reliance on lipreading; the other makes use of sign language as well, and is known technically as "total communication." The "speaker" holds his or her hands up and moves the fingers in a kind of code; the "listener" watches and reads the message. In some schools, sign language is used together with auditory training; in others, it isn't used at all. Parents have the right to choose either method for their child.

In a "combined" lesson in social studies, Ellen used a map of the United States and asked her class to "plan a trip" across the country. The children used both speech and sign language to choose a route while Ellen traced it on the map.

In classes where sign language isn't used, each child is provided with a hearing aid, and the teacher does a lot of talking, speaking loudly and clearly.

The preparation for a teacher of the deaf is to take regular undergraduate college courses, possibly with emphasis on social studies. The Special Education courses in the training of the deaf are taken for the master's degree. These include psychology of the handicapped child, practice in teaching deaf children, the teaching of speech and language to the deaf, and science courses about speech and hearing.

The Clarke School for the Deaf, a private school connected with Smith College, at Northampton, Massachusetts, is one of the best institutions of this type.

TEACHER OF THE HOMEBOUND

The teacher of the homebound deals with children who are physically unable to go to regular school classes. The teacher literally brings the school into the home. It's a very personal and intimate relationship, for the instruction is entirely individual. The teacher has to adjust to the physical, emotional, and social needs of the child.

Teaching the homebound is one of the most interesting and satisfying parts of the program for the handicapped, for it brings the teacher in direct contact with the home and the parents. The teacher not only teaches the child the elementary subjects but often has a good influence on the home atmosphere. With a little thought, a wholesome and cheerful atmosphere can be created for the handicapped child.

[21]

When Edna Weldon, a newly appointed teacher of the homebound, visited the Berner home for the first time, she found that her pupil was a six-year-old girl named Julia who could neither walk properly nor speak clearly. When Julia saw the teacher, she was frightened. With smiles and friendly words, Edna gradually won her over. Julia liked to play with dolls, feeding them and putting them to bed. She spoke to them, too. Although her speech wasn't clear, her babbling varied in tone, showing her different emotions.

What Edna found significant was Julia's attitude toward her dolls. It was definitely not friendly. Every time a doll toppled over, Julia would set it up again with a slap and hostile grunt. Edna soon discovered that this was the very way Julia was treated by her own mother. This treatment had built up a resentful feeling in Julia toward her mother. Edna counseled Julia's mother and helped her learn to use more loving ways with the child.

Edna also helped to change Julia's attitude by expressing sympathy for the doll. Every time Julia struck the doll, Edna took it, fondled it in her arms, and said, "Don't cry, you poor thing; Julia didn't mean it," and pretended to wipe tears from its face. Julia gradually stopped slapping her doll and when it fell, she picked it up and comforted it.

Speaking slowly and distinctly, Edna was able to get Julia to imitate her and to enunciate clearly. She aroused the little girl's interest and got her to put forth more effort by praising her generously. Every time Edna came, she brought Julia a flower or picture, and the child looked forward to her sessions with the teacher.

After a while, Julia's condition improved, in every way. Her body control became better and she smiled at her mother and teacher.

A teacher of the homebound is now a regular member of the staff of every well-organized program for the handicapped.

The requirements for a license as teacher of the homebound include a B.A. degree, and practice in the teaching of handicapped children, or special courses in the teaching of physically and emotionally handicapped children.

RESOURCE TEACHER

The resource teacher is in charge of a room with special equipment, teaching materials, and books, to which pupils go who need individual instruction and guidance. They may be visually impaired, multiple-handicapped, or hard-of-hearing.

Many of these children are not segregated. They share in regular class activities, but they also receive individual help several times a week from the resource teacher. She or he takes care of visually limited and hard-of-hearing children who are able to read printed materials and can move around in regular classes and who have normal mentality.

The resource room has all kinds of recorded material (phonograph records or cassettes) and tactile material like Braille. This is the system of raised symbols which the blind can read by touch. The resource teacher gives them extra help. She or he also deals with children who are mentally retarded or emotionally disturbed.

The resource room for the visually handicapped contains books printed in large type, optical devices,

---

Overleaf: Teachers and teachers' aides provide the close, personal attention that helps these handicapped children to learn and grow.

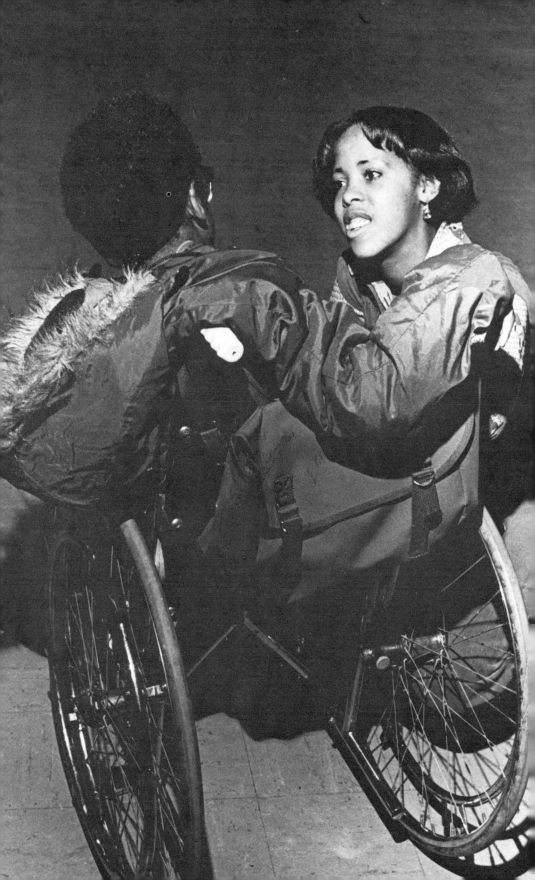

magnifiers, a tape recorder, a TV set, and a typewriter with large type.

The requirements for resource teaching are a B.A. degree and courses in education, elementary school methods, child psychology, and teaching the handicapped.

TEACHER OF THE MULTIPLE-HANDICAPPED

"Yes," says Anne Potter, a school psychologist at the Center for Multiple-Handicapped Children in New York City, "it seemed too much to ask of one small special school, to take children who couldn't walk, who couldn't talk, some who couldn't see, couldn't hear, couldn't learn, couldn't sit still, couldn't relate, and just couldn't make it in any other school setting."

Children from four to eighteen, whose intelligence ranged all the way from low to high; children with almost every type of sensory and motor handicap; blind and deaf, paralyzed, hyperactive, brain-injured children were to be grouped according to disability. The school psychologists looked upon the project with considerable misgivings. And yet it has been tremendously successful. Anne Potter adds:

"Last year we graduated fully one-fourth of our student population. They went on to all sorts of special educational settings. Several of our older children went into vocational training programs. Yet many of these same children had previously been unable to qualify for these classes or had been unable to adjust in them.

"Tommy, for example, is deaf and came to us with little speech. He had been unable to make it in a school for the deaf because of his angry, aggressive, difficult behavior. He is back there now and doing well.

"Or Pedro, an appealing mite of a five-year-old deaf, cerebral-palsied boy with a charming grin. He could barely crawl when he entered the Center and had no speech. By last spring, he was scuttling down the hall on crutches and speaking in short phrases. He is now in a school for the deaf and one of their favorites.

"Of the thirty or more graduates of the last two years, all but two are doing well. This is, however, but one side of the picture. More important are the intangibles, which have been developed in the children—self-confidence, sense of personal worth, the essence of what makes life worthwhile. These children have come to feel that there is a place in the world for them. . . . One feels it immediately in watching the children's faces light up with pride when they master a task in the classroom, or in the happy noisy scramble down the halls for lunch . . . and especially does one feel it in the assemblies, in the enormous joy and pride the children display when they are putting on a play or singing a song for their schoolmates.

"To put it a bit more professionally: The greatest gains shown by our children have been in the areas of personality development, ego growth, and self-concept."

Although students in the classes for the multiple-handicapped vary greatly in age and handicaps, their individual needs are provided for as far as possible. The children are reached through a great variety of approaches. Many students are retarded mentally, and they have to be taught the most elementary concepts, such as shape and color. The teacher has to do many tasks at once. For instance, in a second-grade class, a youngster was stringing beads of three colors according to a pattern that the teacher had given him. He was working diligently at this and the teacher gave him continual encouragement.

Meanwhile, the boy next to him began chewing the beads. The teacher started him on a different project and then gave her attention to a little girl who was trying to put objects of different shapes into the corresponding

openings of a box. Next to her sat a youngster who was trying to draw with crayons. On the floor lay three children playing with toys. One had a toy lion; the other two were playing with toy telephones. They were all learning about "communicating." Lying on the floor with them was a student teacher from a university, talking to them and guiding them.

The teachers were kept busy dashing from one youngster to the other, helping, commenting, criticizing, and praising. This kind of teaching demands endless imagination, sympathy, and energy as well as training.

The requirements for the license to teach multiple-handicapped pupils are a B.A. degree and courses in the psychology of the mentally retarded, mental and educational measurements, teaching the multiple-handicapped, and creative arts for children.

TEACHER OF MENTALLY RETARDED CHILDREN

The teacher of children with retarded mental development (CRMD) has the delicate task of changing the mindset and attitude of the retarded child so that he does not feel unhappy or unwanted at school. In other words, guiding the child's behavior is more important than teaching subject matter. Feelings and spirit must be influenced; character is to be formed and strengthened.

"These children," says Elizabeth Burton, a school psychologist, "come to us with profoundly damaged self-concepts. We are happy to say that we have created

---

Song period becomes a chance
to work with speech at These
Our Treasures Day Care
Center (TOTS) in New York.

an atmosphere of warmth in which they gain a feeling of importance, of being cared for, of being loved. In short, they come to feel that they have a place in the world and that the world has a place for them."

The CRMD teacher tries to see that the classroom activities are interesting and fun. Much paper work, coloring, and drawing is used in teaching all subjects from reading to history, geography, and nature study.

Since retarded children need help in all aspects of life, including family life, they learn about various household activities. For this purpose, usually a room called the "Home Living Room" is provided. It contains a complete set of dining room, bedroom, and living room furniture, and kitchen equipment. There, the children can act out different household activities.

In a cooking lesson, for instance, various members of the class share different activities. Joan, the teacher, moves about and talks continually. The most elementary operations are discussed and then performed by different pupils. The whole group may come over to the stove to watch one of the pupils move a pot. Joan asks: "Where is the pot? How is it? How do you know it is hot? How should you move it?"

While one child volunteers to cover the table with paper from a large roll, Joan may produce a basket filled with utensils or vegetables. She will show these and ask questions about them. "How many carrots do we have? Count them, Olga. What must we do? How can we clean them?"

_____

A teacher at TOTS
and a mentally
handicapped child
enjoy a story together.

Joan will show how to cut off the tip of the carrot and she will let several pupils do it themselves. Holding up a head of lettuce, she will ask: "What must we do first? How do we separate it?" One pupil will handle the lettuce while others peel the carrots.

All of these elementary operations are explained in detail and carried out slowly. Each child participates, some with greater skill than others. Both boys and girls take part. Joan asks many questions. She insists on complete sentences for the answers.

Much of the instruction of retarded children is individual. At any time, there will be as many different activities as there are children in the classroom. For example, in a room of severely mentally retarded children, the following "reading" activities may be going on at the same time:

One pupil has two sets of cards. One set consists of pictures of objects, the other of cards with their names in neat type. The aim of the pupil is to place the appropriate word under each picture. These are easily recognizable—bird, horse, house, automobile, and so on.

At another table, two children look at cards on each of which appears a capital letter and the picture of an object whose name begins with that letter (B—banana; N—nest; M—monkey). One youngster pronounces each letter as he looks at it. The other child who is less disabled, helps his classmate and corrects him when he makes a mistake.

At a third table, a girl is placing printed slips, each containing one word, in piles according to the first letter (tree, toe, tongue, teeth; horse, house, hood, and so on).

Another youngster is busy fitting together cards that contain pictures of objects and animals, so that the two will rhyme (mop—top; bell—well; pail—nail; cat—bat;

fox—box). At another table, a boy has a set of playing cards. He arranges these in descending order (king, queen, jack, 10, 9, and so on).

Meanwhile, the teacher moves from one child to another, commenting, assisting, correcting, and praising. This job, though specialized, is similar to others already described for which the teacher needs patience and skill.

The requirements for a license to teach retarded children are a B.A. degree, courses having to do specifically with the mentally retarded, and courses in creative arts for children.

BILINGUAL TEACHER

A rapidly expanding educational area is that of bilingual education. It began as a help to normal children speaking a foreign language. Soon it was discovered that there were large numbers of handicapped children who also need this service, so extensive programs in the bigger cities have been provided for them. The federal government is giving these programs generous financial support.

The bilingual teacher teaches the common school subjects to the children in their own languages. The most widely represented foreign languages in the United States are Spanish, Italian, Greek, French, and Chinese. Because of the large number of Hispanics in the United States, the leading language here is Spanish. In Canada, teachers must be bilingual in French and English, especially in Quebec and Ontario.

The children are divided into two groups. One group consists of those who are most limited in English-speaking ability. They take part in activities such as physical training, lunch, art, and music with their English-speaking classmates. They receive bilingual instruction every day in language-arts and math, as well as English as a second language.

The other group consists of those children who are able to speak English fairly well, but are still in need of a bilingual instructional program. They take part in most of the regular class activities, including English as a second language, language arts, and math. They also receive bilingual instruction three times a week in related subjects. The bilingual resource teacher and para-professional aide also teach the history and culture of the particular ethnic group.

The bilingual teacher must have an elementary school license and must be fluent in the foreign language, which is his or her specialty.

Paraprofessionals

1975126

The paraprofessional is a teacher or an assistant teacher or aide who hasn't yet completed all the requirements for a professional license. Most paraprofessionals take courses while on the job and thus prepare themselves for a higher position in the school system.

The paraprofessional may work with the children in all the elementary subjects, but particularly in reading, spelling, and arithmetic. Usually, the paraprofessional deals with the children in smaller groups and tries to identify with their particular needs. She or he works,

Overleaf: A paraprofessional
has varied duties. Here,
a paraprofessional teaches
a child to recognize colors,
and then helps to serve meals.

of course, in close contact with the regular classroom teacher.

On the high school level, paraprofessionals do less teaching, although they may do some remedial teaching. Some of the assignments are nonteaching, such as clerical duties in the office, operating duplicating machines, taking care of audio-visual equipment, serving in the library, and working in the stockroom.

The requirements for the position of paraprofessional vary in different states and cities. In general, a high school diploma and a year or two of college, with emphasis on elementary school methods, is enough.

The salary range is from $8,000 to $15,000.

Speech
Therapist

The speech therapist is also known as teacher of speech improvement, or speech pathologist. He or she deals with children who have speech or language defects and also with the hard-of-hearing. Special techniques are used for lipreading, oral exercises, and correction of speech. The speech therapist evaluates, tests, and provides remedial treatment for physical and psychological speech disorders.

At present, the speech therapist is someone who has satisfied state requirements for providing speech therapy in a public school setting.

The field is growing, but right now the situation is somewhat tight in metropolitan areas and particularly throughout the East. In the less populated and rural areas, the prospects for employment are brighter.

A B.A. degree at least is required and most states require an M.A. in speech pathology. The requirements include courses in speech and hearing fundamentals and

speech correction, courses in education, and a year of clinical experience.

The salary range is from $9,000 to $25,000. It varies, however, from one section of the country to the other. It also varies with the setting—public school, hospital, or clinic. Many therapists engage in private practice on the side, which adds to their income.

Young mentally-handicapped children often do not know how to use their jaw muscles; the first step for a speech therapist may be to start a feeding program. While slowly introducing solid foods, the teacher shows the child how to control her jaws. A student teacher who will give daily feedings watches.

Clinical Audiologist

The audiologist (hearing expert) generally specializes only in those disorders that involve loss of hearing so great that it affects speech. There are separate licenses for a clinical audiologist and speech therapist. The two are separate but related occupations.

The requirements for audiologist include the B.A. degree; courses in clinical methods, educational psychology, speech and hearing fundamentals, hearing problems, oral interpretation, and practice in speech correction; and a year of clinical experience.

The audiologist takes more courses and receives

In a speech training program, a Gallaudet College graduate student works with a child who is hard-of-hearing.

more intensive training in audiology (hearing) than the speech pathologist.

The salary range is from $9,000 to $25,000.

A detailed and complete outline of courses and academic preparation is given in a booklet ("Handbook of Audiology") published by the American Speech and Hearing Association (ASHA), 9030 Old Georgetown Road, Washington, D.C. 20014.

Some Related Fields

Although these specialized professions are really separate from the field of Special Education, they are mentioned here because they play an important role in helping handicapped children.

The **guidance counselor** engages in a wide variety of activities. These include going over reports, records, and referrals of the child; giving group guidance lessons and individual or group tests; arranging for visits of parents and pupils to high schools; arranging interviews and meetings to discuss problems of a given child; keep-

Overleaf: Learning the coordination to handle everyday tasks is an important achievement. While Kim teaches a mentally handicapped little girl how to pour, Anthony takes a short break.

ing files for all the children; leading parents' groups; helping the staff to get along together; going to faculty meetings; helping design the program to meet individual needs; and working together with the community and its social agencies.

Through these various activities, the guidance counselor serves the child, the teacher, the parent, and the community.

It is the counselor who acts primarily as the connecting link between the child and other school personnel and the family. Many of the children are in regular medical programs at hospitals and clinics. The counselor keeps these agencies aware of the child's progress and needs. Working with teachers, parents, and outside agencies, the guidance counselor helps to develop the child's potential—academically, socially, and emotionally. Some guidance counselors are specially trained to deal with the handicapped.

The requirements for the license are a B.A. degree and courses in the field of school counseling, including supervised practice in guidance.

The **bilingual guidance counselor** deals with children whose mother tongue is a foreign language and who have difficulty in expressing themselves in English. Various languages are included in this program. The most widely represented are Spanish, Italian, French, Greek, and Chinese. The languages vary in different parts of the country, depending upon the ethnic groups in the com-

---

A physically handicapped
child visits with a
counselor who keeps
constant track of the
child's progress and needs.

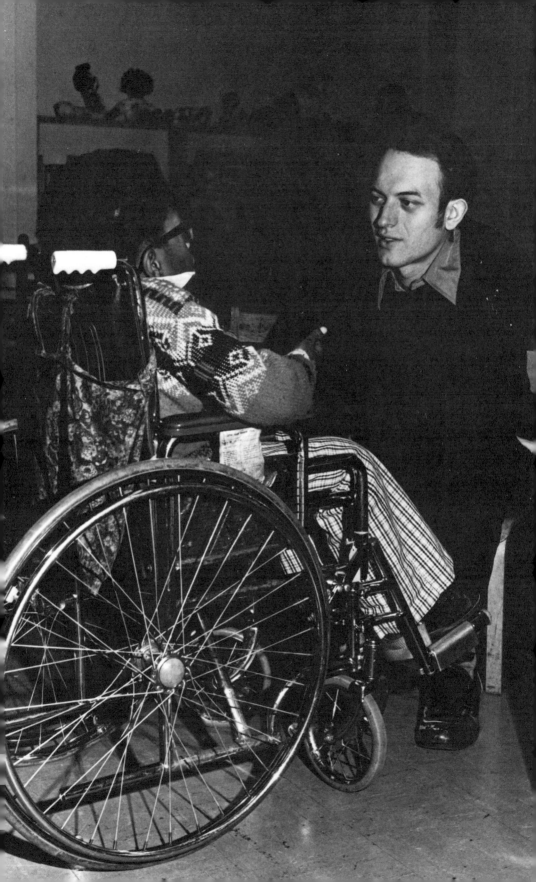

munity. In Philadelphia, for instance, Korean is taught; in Chicago, there are classes in Polish.

The preparation for the license includes the B.A. degree and graduate study in the field of school counseling, as well as supervised practice in guidance. In some systems, two years of experience as a teacher or a bilingual teacher are required, as well as background in guidance and counseling, such as experience as a family caseworker, social worker, fieldworker in human relations, or youth bureau worker.

The bilingual guidance counselor advises, guides, counsels, and helps the child speaking a foreign language. He or she aids the child in school studies, and acts as a liaison between home and school. Because of the large number of Hispanics in some of the larger cities, Spanish is the predominant language. French is used in the East chiefly with Haitian children, and, of course, in Canada.

The salary range for these counselors is from $9,000 to $20,000.

The **school psychologist** uses tests and interviews to evaluate the capacities of a child and then recommends placement in a school or special treatment. Later on, he or she may be called in by the principal, teacher, or parent if special problems arise, particularly with emotionally disturbed children. The psychologist holds a master's degree.

The **school psychiatrist** takes care of the more severe cases of emotional disturbance which call for treatment or therapy. The psychiatrist is a registered M.D. and the holder of a license to practice medicine as well as psychiatry.

The **social worker** gathers information about the child and the child's family. It is the social worker who deals primarily with the parents, getting information from them that is valuable in placing the child. After the child has been admitted to a special school or center, the social worker continues working individually with the child and the parents. The social worker also acts as the liaison between the school and the parents' association.

Your Future in Special Education

Due to the economic recession, many school budgets throughout the country are cut. The tendency is to drop the subjects considered least important. However, Special Education is definitely not in this category. More and more, it is realized how urgent the need is for the training of countless handicapped children. The federal government and state governments are increasing their allotments for this program. According to recent legislation, the grants rise from 5 percent the first year (beginning 1 October 1977) to 40 percent in 1982. New York City would get $8 million in 1977 and double that amount in 1978.

Most of the areas of Special Education are promising, especially education of the blind, the deaf, and the multiple-handicapped.

If you are interested in Special Education, you shouldn't hesitate to enter this attractive field of education and make it your life's work.

Appendix

OPPORTUNITIES IN SOME CITIES

All of the larger cities of the country maintain divisions in their school systems for the education of the handicapped. The job titles may vary, but the subdivisions and the activities are pretty much alike.

Philadelphia

In Philadelphia, programs for the handicapped are classified in the following categories: individual development, hospital, emotionally disturbed, remedial disciplinary, retarded trainable, hearing handicapped, visually handicapped, homebound, learning disability, and orthopedic. Almost twelve thousand children are involved in the different programs.

The salaries are: B.A., $8,900–$17,161; M.A., $9,200–$19,432; M.S. plus thirty credits, $9,780–$20,960; Ph.D., $10,380–$22,600.

San Francisco

The San Francisco school system provides programs for the trainable mentally retarded, pupils with severe language disability, multiple-handicapped, physically handicapped, impaired hearing, visually handicapped, and orthopedic. There is also a program in which mildly handicapped children are placed in separate classes without the use of the word "handicapped," so as to avoid being "labeled." Another interesting program is that of teaching homebound children—and some children in class—by telephone.

For all of these programs, an extensive staff is required, which includes specially licensed teachers, psychologists, therapists, resource teachers, social workers, and paraprofessionals.

Chicago

The Chicago program for the handicapped is known as EMH—educable mentally handicapped. Teachers in this program must meet the academic requirements for a regular Chicago teaching certificate, the state requirements for Special Education (EMH), and sixteen hours in the field of mental retardation. About ten thousand children are involved in Special Education in Chicago.

The administrative offices of the Chicago Board of Education are at 228 North La Salle Street, Chicago, Illinois 60601, Elberta E. Pruitt, Director of Special Education.

Boston

The Boston public schools have seven thousand children in Special Education. The address of the offices is: Boston Public Schools, 15 Beacon Street, Boston, Massachusetts 02108.

The Massachusetts Department of Education, Division of Special Education, 182 Tremont Street, Boston, Massachusetts 02111, maintains a program known as "766." This refers to a chapter of that number in the Education Act. About one hundred thousand children in Massachusetts have "special educational needs."

Cleveland
The Cleveland Board of Education, Division of Special Education, 1380 East 6th Street, Cleveland, Ohio 44114, maintains seven programs which are funded under Title III of the Elementary and Secondary Education Act. These are speech therapy, work-study, elementary and mentally retarded (EMR), learning behaviorally disabled (LBD), crippled children, visually impaired, and hearing impaired.

Los Angeles
The Los Angeles Unified School District publishes a bulletin of ninety-four pages on Special Education entitled, "We Serve the Exceptional Child." In the Unified School District, there are twenty-one special schools exclusively for "identified handicaps," numerous special classes in regular schools, six diagnostic centers for the educationally handicapped, and seven development centers for multiple-handicapped minors. For children confined to their homes, there are tele-classes and itinerant teachers. There is also a program in driver education.

Special Education is under the direction of the Division of Special Education at the Los Angeles Board of Education, 450 North Grand Avenue, Los Angeles, California 90012.

A complete list of publications of the State Department of Education may be obtained from the California State Department of Education, 721 Capitol Mall, Sacramento, California 95814.

New York

With a staff of six thousand, the New York City school system maintains the largest department for the education of the handicapped. Of the more than 90,000 retarded children served, about 50,000 are moderately speech-handicapped. They attend regular schools and get services from resource teachers. More than 12,500 retarded children are waiting to be placed. In 1975, the New York schools spent $193.5 million for the education of the handicapped.

With the $15 million granted by the federal government for the education of the handicapped, the school authorities have organized twenty-four programs. The staff consists of 908 professionally trained persons, including guidance counselors, educational associates, supervisors, secretaries, coordinators, and social workers. In addition, there are 171 paraprofessionals.

Some of the programs are modest, being conducted in small centers with a personnel of three or four teachers. Others, like the Supplementary Reading Program for Handicapped Children, are extensive. This particular program is conducted in fifty-seven schools throughout the city and involves 2,325 handicapped pupils between the ages of five and sixteen. They include 780 minimally brain-injured and physically handicapped, 330 emotionally handicapped, 915 mentally retarded, and 300 emotionally disturbed children. Another elaborate program is one for multiple-handicapped pupils which the federal government has granted $359,239. The children in this program are the severely educationally deprived.

At stated intervals, the Board of Examiners announces examinations for licenses as teachers of the blind, of children with limited vision, of health conservation, of the deaf and hard-of-hearing, and of children with retarded mental development (CRMD).

Holders of licenses may be assigned to elementary schools, junior high schools, or senior high schools. Health conservation teachers may also be called upon to teach in hospitals and convalescent homes.

As stated before, a license to teach the handicapped requires a B.A. degree plus courses in the history and principles of education, elementary methods, practice teaching, child psychology, together with courses preparing for the special category—teaching of the deaf, blind, homebound, and so on.

Salaries range from $9,600 to $20,000 in sixteen salary steps. An additional compensation of $200 is given teachers of the handicapped.

The Board of Education of New York City, 110 Livingston Street, Brooklyn, New York 11201, issues the following publications:

"The Establishment of a Center for Multiple-Handicapped Children"

"Federally Funded Programs"

"Brief History of the Bureau for Children with Retarded Mental Development"

"Individual Pupil Profile"

"Division of Special Education—Directory of Services"

OPPORTUNITIES IN CANADA

As in the United States, the area of education of the handicapped is expanding rapidly in Canada and there are many positions for qualified persons. According to the *Canada Year Book,* 1975: "There is an increasing interest in the education of exceptional children. New types of special classes are sometimes started by parents of children with a common disability. . . . Progress in providing such education varies from province to province and is most commonly found in city school systems."

The *Directory of Associations in Canada* (Brian Land, University of Toronto Press, 1975), lists eighty-one associations interested in the education of the handicapped.

In general, Canada is not yet as advanced in this field as the United States. Standards vary from province to province and are higher in the cities than in the rural areas. For the most part, requirements are less severe than in the States.

One Canadian educator, in commenting on the present state of affairs, stresses the need for more qualified personnel:

"There is also a chronic shortage of competent qualified personnel in the area of consultants in special services, of people such as school psychologists, reading specialists, speech therapists, audiologists, and elementary school counselors." (Stanley Perkins, "Shortcomings in the Delivery of Special Education," *Education Canada*, Spring 1975, p. 21).

Some advance has been made in setting up a network of Special Education Instructional Material Centers. Also more paraprofessionals are being employed. That the need is great can be seen from a recent report that there are a million children in Canada with emotional and learning disorders.

The language of instruction in Quebec is, of course, French. A knowledge of this language is also useful in Ontario.

ASSOCIATIONS AND AGENCIES

The *Encyclopedia of Associations* provides the names of state and private associations for the handicapped and retarded in the United States.

Some Canadian Associations are listed below:

Canada Education Association
252 Bloor St., W
Toronto, Ont. M5S IV5

Metropolitan Toronto Association
for Mentally Retarded
30 Birch Ave.
Toronto, Ont. M4V IC8

Ottawa Association
for Mentally Retarded
31 Spadina Ave.
Ottawa, Ont. K1Y 2B8

Kootenay Society
for the Handicapped
Box 1427
Creston, B.C. V0B IG0

North Shore Association
for the Mentally Retarded
3069 Lonsdale Ave.
North Vancouver, B.C. V7N 3J6

Vancouver-Richmond Association
for the Mentally Retarded
1071 S.E. Marine Dr.
Vancouver, B.C. V5X 2V5

Greater Victoria Association
for the Retarded
631 Fort St. #3
Victoria, B.C. V8W IGI

NATIONAL HEADQUARTERS OF CRIPPLED CHILDREN'S AGENCIES

Foundation for Child Development
345 E. 46th St., New York, N.Y. 10017

Muscular Dystrophy Association
of America
157 W. 57th St., New York, N.Y. 10019

Myasthenia Gravis Foundation
230 Park Ave., New York, N.Y. 10017

National Association
for Retarded Citizens
420 Lexington Ave.,
New York, N.Y. 10017

National Foundation
600 Third Ave., New York, N.Y. 10016

National Foundation for Genetics
and Neuromuscular Diseases
250 W. 57th St., New York, N.Y. 10019

National Multiple Sclerosis Society
205 E. 42nd St., New York, N.Y. 10017

National Easter Seal Society
for Crippled Children and Adults
2023 West Ogden Ave.,
Chicago, Ill. 60612

United Cerebral Palsy
Association, Inc.
66 E. 34th St., New York, N.Y. 10016

Index

About the Author

Dr. Huebener was born and brought up in New York City. He attended public schools and City College. He has a Master's Degree from Columbia and a Ph.D. from Yale.

The author has taught on every level, from grade-school to university. He was Director of Foreign Languages in the New York City schools for over 20 years and has been a lecturer at City College, Hunter, and N.Y.U.

Dr. Huebener has also traveled widely. He was Consultant in Education for the State Department in its Re-education Program in West Germany in 1950 and 1951. He is a member of the Bureau of Overseas Speakers of the State Department. He has lectured in France, Holland, West Germany, East Germany, Switzerland, Austria, Ethiopia, and South Africa. In May, 1976, he spoke at the University of Heidelberg.

At present, Dr. Huebener is Supervisor of Student Teachers in the School of Education of New York University.